PRAIRIE FIRES
AND
PAPER MOONS

PRAIRIE FIRES AND PAPER MOONS

The American Photographic Postcard: 1900–1920

HAL MORGAN AND ANDREAS BROWN
FOREWORD BY JOHN BASKIN

David R. Godine ★ Publisher ★ Boston

First published in 1981 by
David R. Godine, Publisher, Inc.
306 Dartmouth Street
Boston, Massachusetts 02116

Library of Congress Cataloging in Publication Data
Morgan, Hal.
    Prairie fires and paper moons.
    1. United States—Description and travel—Views.
2. United States—Social life and customs—1865–1918—
Pictorial works. 3. Postal cards—United States.
I. Brown, Andreas. II. Title.
E168.M838   973.91   81-47327
ISBN 0-87923-404-0   AACR2

Design and production by Hal Morgan, Inc., Cambridge,
Massachusetts

MANUFACTURED IN THE UNITED STATES OF AMERICA

First printing August 1981

PHOTOGRAPH CREDITS

The photographs in this book are from the collection of
the Gotham Book Mart, Inc., New York City, with the ex-
ception of those listed below which appear by permission
of the lenders:

Henry Deeks: 96 left, 97 bottom, 101 left, 102 left.
David Freund: 39, 133 top, 140 right, 144, 161, 170 bot-
    tom.
Rusty Kane: 10 bottom.
Ron Menchine: 100 top, 102 right.
The Metropolitan Museum of Art, The Jefferson Burdick
    Collection: 5 left, 28 right, 34 top and bottom, 42 top,
    47 top, 113 left and right, 120.
Mrs. Nellie (C. B.) Micklea: 25 top, 65 bottom, 80 bottom,
    82 top, 124, 133 bottom, 135 top, 146.
Dr. George Miller: 74, 89, 179.
Hal Morgan: 7 left, 45 bottom, 119 bottom, 123, 160 bot-
    tom.
Weston Naef: ii, 43, 131.
Marion Perkins: 127.
William Peterson: 126 top.
Don Preziosi and Newly West: 16 left and right, 20 left, 36
    top, 44, 45 top, 56 top, 57, 68, 112, 118, 132, 151, 165,
    178 top.
José Rodriguez: 77 bottom.
Leah Schnall: 130 bottom.
Sam Wagstaff: 15 left.

Contents

Postcard portrait made at Rensler's Studio,
Cincinnati, Ohio.

Foreword

THE BAKERS WERE AN OLD FAMILY, which ran down on the dry prospects of two sons confirmed into a bachelorhood as staunch as their Republicanism. I discovered them in the basement of my farmhouse, in a mildewed box of old diaries and postcards. The elder son's prose was a combination of droll, self-deprecatory humor and a perpetual, grousing feud with all of nature, which he nonetheless respected even as he saw the rain falling on his neighbor's corn while his own parched in the July heat. Between that and the old sepia postcards, I soon felt I knew them at least as well as my own remote kin.

The postcards were scattered randomly throughout the diaries and tumbled startlingly out from between Ralph Baker's days. His parents, John and Martha, were photographed on the porch. John Baker was seated in a plain cane-bottom kitchen chair, dressed in his Sunday coat, vest, and tie, but wearing work pants and heavy field shoes. Martha stood behind him, in a long dark skirt and white blouse. She wore glasses; he wore a thick, graying mustache.

Her eyes were wide open, unnaturally so, and her scant smile was the thin smile of civilization and not much more—the arbitrary gesture of cautious people meeting others for the first time. He was sleepy-eyed, his arms folded as if he were husbanding his strength, which is not to say that he had none for though he was wizened and old, he was not weak. Behind them on the porch was a clothesline, and on it, billowing faintly, were lace curtains, which somehow gave the photograph a slightly haunted look, although it was not a haunting in the sense of the supernatural, but rather an evocation of light, air, and space, as well as of time itself.

The sons would not hold for such scrutiny. They lurked around the edges of the cards, in groups where they stared, solemn and luminous-eyed, from under wide-brimmed hats and in shots of people at work, where they hung back and let the teams of horses or the miraculous, evolving machinery claim the camera's full attention.

I loved the old cards. I had never seen such curious items before. My family maintained albums of old photographs, but the postcards in my mother's hatbox were either plain or the beamy pastels of mountain scenery and Florida beaches. It was not in our tradition to publicly mail our relatives around the countryside.

So I dealt out the Baker postcards on my work table and speculated on them. There were family gatherings, work scenes, couples and threesomes in formal attitudes on porches and in yards, even a dim photograph of a dormitory room at Ohio State, where one of the cousins went to school. Most of the cards seemed to be extra copies, pristine, not mailed, without messages—only the printed label: POST CARD.

I began to collect old photographs of my neighborhood, particularly of the first two or three decades of the century, and I discovered that many of these images, too, were made as postcards. From my clumsy survey of that time, there seemed to have been as many negatives made into postcards as into regular photographs. I could picture them fluttering into the new mailboxes over the countryside, when everything must have felt novel, even motion, and imagery itself.

People were new to each other. As late as 1850, a French artist did colored lithographs of New York that included temples, palaces, minarets, pagodas, and pyramids among the city buildings, and people wearing fezzes, coolie hats, Chinese gowns, saris, and top hats. These views were made to calm the fears of Frenchmen coming to work America's goldfields. At a lesser distance and likely a later time, New England fishermen were not absolutely certain what Ohio farmers looked like, as they peered curiously and somewhat suspiciously over the horizon at each other.

Photography was recent, an industrial invention. This creation by Niepce and Daguerre dated from 1839, the year a German newspaper, recognizing that something formidable was in the works, wrote: "God would have to betray all his Eternal Principles to allow a Frenchman in Paris to unleash such a diabolic invention upon the world." It is hard to tell how much of that was aimed at the French and how much at the idea of man's effrontery in trying to build a machine that would capture, in a mechanical process, the image of God. Even so, for a significant part of the nineteenth century, imagery still belonged to painters, novelists, and nature.

The personal American photographic postcard had several nineteenth-century predecessors, the daguerreotype and the stereograph being my own favorites. The old daguerreotype portraits, for all their samenesses, still have a power about them. There is, in these old photographs, rage and pride, fierceness and failure, and, in many, something of a subtle but nonetheless wild-eyed look as though the subjects were sitting under duress, ready to bolt if the process turned painful, which they fully expected.

The stereographs—two similar images mounted side by side to fit in a stereoscopic viewer—came along after the Civil War and persisted through the time of the personal photographic postcard, but people were still suspicious of the process. Some of the early stereographs carried a written affirmation: "I have looked these views carefully over and find them very correct. I was present when they were taken. The pictures and statuary are in their original places." Then it was signed by the witness. One picture was not yet worth a thousand words, but photography was on its way toward making people think such a simple-minded sentiment *might* be true.

The curious—and who would not admit to the virtue of curiosity?—began to study the newly photographed world and draw a few rudimentary conclusions. Oliver Wendell Holmes, who invented the hand stereoscope, noted that no matter where in the world his stereographs came from, the clothesline seemed to be somewhere present. Mr. Holmes's judgment was that the clothesline was pertinent to what he called "the decencies of civilization," and he thereby set himself up as one of the first sociologists.

In one of her short stories, Eudora Welty describes looking into the stereoscope, and it is likely that many viewers felt precisely so:

> We passed each other those sand-pink cities and passionate fountains, the waterfall that rocks snuffed out like a light, islands in the sea, red pyramids, sleeping towers, checkered pavements on which strollers had come out, with shadows that seemed to steal further each time, as if the strollers had moved, and where the statues had rainbow edges; volcanoes, the Sphinx, and Constantinople; and again the Lakes, like starry fields— brought forward each time so close that it seemed to me the tracings from the beautiful face of a strange coin were being laid against my brain.

Soon, photographers would confirm the worst fears of that old German editorialist. These practitioners were not only going casually after the image of God, they were taking on all of nature. "Let me advise you here to always have with you on your photographic trips, a spade and a good axe," wrote photographer James Mullen in 1874. "I remember on one occasion finding it necessary to cut down four large forest trees, in order to get a view of a peculiar formation of rock-work. . . ."

In 1888, George Eastman marketed a camera that contained a hundred snapshots. When these had been exposed, the camera was mailed back to the company and for $10 (not an insignificant sum, by the way) the pictures were developed, the camera reloaded, and everything returned to the owner. This, of course, prepared the way for the camera to become an amateur's machine. The commercial photographers would soon suffer like the portrait painters before them, and, in the not-so-distant future, they would all be saved by the invention of advertising. But what Eastman's work did immediately was encourage photographic democracy. In the hands of everyman, photography relaxed a bit more, bestowing the mixed blessing that marks every form of democracy. The personal photographic postcards were a direct, if somewhat marginal, result of Mr. Eastman's entrepreneurship.

The simple nature of photography made it increasingly accessible. Even in its first difficult forms, photography had a populist air about it. James F. Ryder, a Cleveland photographer, wrote that it was not uncommon to find watch repairers, dentists, and other business folk making daguerreotypes as a sideline. "I have known blacksmiths and cobblers to double up with it," he said, "so it was possible to have a horse shod, your boots tapped, a tooth pulled, or a likeness taken by the same man."

Consider what was occurring in America in the years around the turn of the century: In the 1890s, the first Ferris wheel was constructed. Libraries expanded. The first subway was built. The zipper was introduced. By 1900, a train had gone seventy-eight miles per hour. In 1903, the Wright brothers flew, and, in 1904, a woman was arrested in New York for smoking a cigarette while riding in an open automobile. Motion in every conceivable way. We were getting on and we were delighted with ourselves. The newly democratized photography could promote us and all our new enthusiasms.

Consider, also, the very size of the country. The place was too big. Too much space, too much silence. Man's nature abhors a vacuum. He would fill it up with *something.* For a time, the motion belonged largely to the cities. By the time it reached the provinces, it had slowed, wound down under the gravity of distance.

Ralph Baker, eighteen years old by 1900 and living nine rural Ohio miles from the county seat, was as isolated as the moons of Saturn. He and Walter, two years younger, were already farming. The postcard photographs showed them as slight of frame but wiry, the type to stay away from in local arm-wrestling contests. Between diary and postcard, I learned that the boys attended church, got into periodic debates held at the schoolhouse, worried about the treachery of Democrats, read a good bit of Emerson—and were somewhat wary of the camera. There is one postcard with Ralph and Walter sheltered amidst a phalanx of relatives and, on the back, a message from Ralph to a cousin telling of going to Cincinnati to hear Eugene Ysaye, the Belgian violinist. "Ysaye lived fully up to his great reputation," read the message. "It was a very fine concert." Then he noted that the train trip of twenty-five miles had cost him $1.60, remarked on the weather (it was clear in the afternoon and fifty degrees), and signed off.

There was no apparent connection between photograph and message, except that both were personal, which is what gave the quirky little era of these postcards the strong character it had. It was a rather brief fad, but a fine one, carrying with it a particular and enviable sense of celebration, as the splendid postcards collected by Hal Morgan and Andreas Brown demonstrate over and over.

Many of the work scenes illustrated in this book are both proud and playful. Consider the scene of the work gang perched like blackbirds up and down the utility pole or that of the barn raising with the men standing along the skeletal bent in various attitudes of swagger. There is a great *connected-ness* in these pictures because the people are involved in what they are doing and because they chose the scenes to represent themselves.

As for the solemnity etched into the faces on the cards, that would persist for a time. Sobriety, after all, was an American virtue, and photography was still a ceremony. A neighborhood child, looking at my old postcards, studied them a long while, her own face as grave as theirs, then said, "It looks as though they never had a red dress. . . ." The solemnity, wrote Alan Thomas, a University of Toronto professor writing about nineteenth-century photography, arose from "the self-consciousness of people aware that they may be exposing themselves to the gaze of their next-door neighbour. The men and women of that century did not, generally speaking, take appearances lightly. . . ."

Mr. Thomas said it was the longer time exposures of the nineteenth century that gave photography "the pace and tone of a ceremony." Time exposures were shortened, but ritual persisted, as it has a way of doing. People in the Bakers' neighborhood were rural folk and, being reminded daily of the rituals in nature, were likely to be influenced by ritual in other places.

Ralph Baker was certainly a man with an eye toward ritual. He lived to be quite old, staying on in the Baker homeplace. Walter died at sixty-five, a victim of heatstroke at harvest time; Ralph found him sitting under the only tree in the grain field where Walter had gone to find shade. Years later, the cousins, as a gift, had a

modern bathroom built onto the house and some months afterward, they noticed the seal had not been broken on the new porcelain toilet bowl. Mr. Baker kept himself to the ritual of the long backyard path.

There were other factors, no doubt, that suggested that committing photography was a serious business. An old resident of my neighborhood, looking through his postcard collection, said he suspects that everyone of that time had bad teeth. An acquaintance in Cincinnati, June Rensler, whose father opened a photographic postcard shop there in 1906, said that people were serious because it is difficult to hold a true smile. She recalls that foreign people, wanting postcard portraits to mail home, favored a sober expression for the camera. "Did they think it made them more intelligent?" she wonders.

Miss Rensler's father was influenced by the exciting field reports of a younger brother who ran away from home to work with a traveling photographer. His response was to open a postcard shop in Over-the-Rhine, the in-town district of brick houses and small shops where most of Cincinnati's sizable German population lived. The location required the Renslers to know German as well as photography.

Part of Mr. Rensler's success with postcards was simply timing. His shop opening happened to coincide with an international epidemic of postcards. The postcard was an idea so simple in conception as to be overlooked, in the way one might overlook a favorite pair of cuff links lying in plain sight on the dresser.

The Viennese postal authorities, impressed by a suggestion from Dr. Emanuel Herrmann, a young economics professor at an Austrian military academy, issued the first government postals in October 1869. The United States brought out its first in 1873. The early cards were plain, but picture cards soon followed, and a simple but large industry, based on imagery and without much regard for nation-state politics, was launched.

In a fabulous sort of way, the position of the postcard was illustrated by an episode in the French film *Les Carabiniers*, in which two peasants join the army, largely because they are promised they can become rich from looting. Years afterward, when they return home, their plunder turns out to be a suitcase filled with hundreds of postcards bearing the images of stores, monuments, nature, and machinery.

The personal photographic postcard had two forms. One was the product of studios like Mr. Rensler's, mostly portraiture, although backdrops were used more and more often for all manner of effect. The other form was the snapshot, taken by amateurs and transferred onto the cards. This was the upstart idea that, finally, shifted the power of the process from the professional to the amateur. Photography by 1900, wrote the photographer Gisele Freund, was no longer "bathed in the mystery of the creative act."

Mr. Rensler, meanwhile, lived on bananas, which were five cents a dozen at the little market up the street, and attended to his craft. He began with nothing, unable to afford all the supplies he needed. When customers lined up on the sidewalk, an assistant collected from everyone, then ran out to buy film. Mr. Rensler considered himself, first, a good businessman. For twenty-five years, he did not have a key to the front door—he was open twenty-four hours a day. He ignored the blue laws, which said he must close on Sunday. On Sundays, he had his assistants run the shop and when they were arrested, he came downtown and bailed them out. He did this until the laws changed. "I wore them out," he told his daughter.

On holidays and many weekends, there were lines down the sidewalk. Halloween was a busy night for the shop. On Halloween, Over-the-Rhine was full of costumed adults, festively roaming the streets, many of them wanting their pictures taken. June, then a young girl, found this somehow frightening: many people were dressed as clowns, but others seemed grotesque. They were good-natured, happy drunks, but to her there was something menacing about adults in costume. Sometimes, she went outside and locked herself in the car.

Many of the same people returned, over and over, to have their photographs made as postcards, in different outfits, with different friends. An old German fellow from the neighborhood came in every weekend. "Mama, no flowers tonight!" he cried, handing Mr. Rensler the last of his money.

Mr. Rensler had different backdrops made for his postcard work. They were done by itinerant painters who were always a little drunk—pale men who worked at night, finishing in the early morning hours like elves and never seen again.

The customers were infatuated with the moon. They sang songs about it, counted the days until it was full again, and wanted their pictures taken with it as a backdrop. It was as though they were noticing it for the first time. So Miss Rensler's grandfather, a contractor, *made* one. It was a great curved sickle of a moon, with a face on it. The customers loved it.

Mr. Rensler considered himself a craftsman as well as a businessman. He trained his daughter as a photographer and would never let her have one of the new box cameras "the little people use," as he put it. Photography was still a respected craft to him, and his customers—particularly the immigrants who did not like to smile for his portraits—treated him respectfully. "Like a doctor," he said.

"Go back and look at the Rembrandts," he told June. "Study the lighting. Photography is all lighting. It is the play of light on a flat surface that gives the illusion of the third dimension. You *must* have shadows. . . ."

The war was as good for the photography shop as it was for other aspects of the economy. The only problem Mr. Rensler had was in finding assistants. He used women and a one-armed man. He estimated that in twenty years he made half a million prints. He built a new house for his family and told them it was made of postcards.

He was a man in the right place at the right time, and the random but coalescing events aided rather than frustrated him. Besides that, he was a man who believed in work. June lay in a hammock, tanning her legs, when he came home and stood beside her. "I love to work," he said and laughed, without judgment. He was one of the restless, driving men who characterized the first part of this century. He also had a hand in shaping this rather odd fad, of people scribbling messages to each other on personal photographs.

I have a neighbor, well into her eighties, who remembers having her picture taken for a postcard. "I looked forward to having my picture taken weeks ahead," she said. "I tried my best to look pretty. I used to grieve because I was not pretty and my father said, 'If you're a good girl, no one will notice.' That was not at all consoling. I did not wish to be good; I wished to be *pretty*. I tried to decide which side was my best, right or left. I decided that because of my hair, my left was more presentable. Then I was at Mr. Howland's studio and I knew that soon I would mail myself off in all my glory to my loved ones. I was nervous. I thought the camera could *catch* me. It seemed so . . . permanent. I would be stopped for one moment and then I would be off in the mails, not to be retrieved again. . . ."

For the Renslers, the postcard business continued until the Second World War. The shop, even today,

looks very much as it did over a half-century ago. Mr. Rensler, who died last year, occupies the window, staring confidently out onto Main Street from one of the few portraits he allowed anyone to take of him. He is wearing a hat and topcoat and jauntily holds a cigar.

"Everything was family," Miss Rensler said. "He wanted us to carry on with the shop, and we did. 'You can trust family,' he said. Then Uncle Will stole from him. 'Well,' he said, 'at least it's family.'" But none of the family photographs seem to have been made into postcards.

Miss Rensler still makes postcards. When the rare occasion calls for one, she cuts up a piece of regular eight-by-ten-inch developing paper. Most of the old backdrops have been given away. The moon wore out.

Just as we can no longer have old-fashioned novels, we can no longer have old-fashioned photographs. It is not the same world. We are scarcely related. These grand postcards were testimony to a distant family, community, time, and space. Mr. Baker stopped having postcards made and became silent, too. In his diaries, in the last years of his life, he recorded only the weather.

The personal photographic postcard was an interesting alloy of several substances and, in all, a fairly remarkable achievement, given man's eager proclivity toward random taste and impersonality. The postcards themselves remain, as one collector said about the daguerreotypes, "potent accessories to slightly melancholic rapture."

JOHN BASKIN
Wilmington, Ohio
March, 1981

xii

Introduction

SEVERAL FACTORS accounted for the popularity of photographic postcards in the years just before the First World War. In 1898, the United States Post Office had announced that Rural Free Delivery of the mail would be provided for groups of farmers who petitioned their congressmen. Until that time, free home delivery had been made only in towns of ten thousand or more residents—roughly twenty-five percent of the country's population. Farmers and other rural people had been required to pick up their mail at the nearest post office, which in many small towns also served as the general store and gathering place.

The change to Rural Free Delivery was not instantaneous, but by 1906 most of the delivery routes had been established, and rural agents were bringing daily mail to isolated homes and farms all across the country. In a few short years, this apparently minor shift in mail delivery policy united the entire nation in an efficient communication network. Previously, many people had made the trip into town for their mail only once a week, but, with the new system in effect, the mail could be counted on to arrive every day, and people began to use the mails differently. Rural daily newspapers experienced a tremendous increase in circulation, and, on a more personal level, an invitation to a Saturday night dance could be mailed safely a day in advance.

In 1898 the Post Office also established a reduced postage rate for privately printed postcards. This ruling, which required that one side of the card be reserved strictly for the address, meant that messages on picture postcards had to be included on the image side of the card. This restriction necessitated blunt correspondence, but, at a penny for postage, communication was cheap. The fever for picture postcards that had already raged for several years in Europe now began to spread to America, where manufacturers started to produce enormous quantities of delicately colored pictures of popular tourist attractions, comic cards, and greetings for special occasions.

In 1902, the Eastman Kodak Company took advantage of the booming international postcard fad by issuing a postcard-size photographic paper on which images could be printed directly from negatives. The Kodak paper and the competing brands that soon filled the market proved to be wildly successful. They allowed parents to make instant portraits of their children, enabled suitors to send photographic remembrances to their sweethearts, and launched professional photographers in the sideline of selling cards illustrating local scenes and events.

These local entrepreneurs soon found that people would pay a little more for postcards of their own small towns and villages—subjects that did not warrant mass production by commercial publishers, but could be profitably produced in limited quantities on photographic postcard stock. As the postcard fad grew, people occasionally asked that their studio portraits be printed as postcards, and some people even hired the photographer to make postcards of their homes and workplaces.

"Gaslight" photographic paper, the kind most commonly used for postcards, was so simple to process that energetic, determined amateurs could make their own prints. Unlike the printing papers of the nineteenth century, which had required exposure in full sunlight, the "gaslight" papers were sensitive enough to be printed at night using artificial light—hence the name. Because the artificial light could be controlled—it was not affected by passing clouds or the time of day—the paper was not only easy to use, but reliable. The most popular brands in the years covered in this book were the Eastman Kodak Company's "Velox" and "Azo," the Defender Photo Supply Company's "Argo," Ansco's "Cyko," and the Artura Paper Company's "Artura."

As the dominant force in the photographic industry, Eastman Kodak also supplied cameras and processing services to amateur postcard makers. The Folding Pocket Kodak no. 3A, which was manufactured in 1903, was designed to take postcard-size negatives (3¼ × 5½ inches). Not until 1909, however, did the company use this feature as a selling point. Between 1906 and 1910, Kodak also promoted the hobby of amateur postcard photography by printing postcards from amateurs' negatives for ten cents a card.

While many photographic postcards were made by amateurs, or from amateurs' negatives—most of the pictures reproduced in this book were made by professionals. After 1907, when the postal law was liberalized to allow messages on the address side of the cards, the production of photographic postcards grew into a substantial business. During the several years before the war, many professional photographers produced almost nothing but postcards.

One lucrative branch of the postcard business was the portrait-studio concession at resorts, amusement parks, and county fairs, where tourists could have comic portraits of themselves made. Photography handbooks published between 1906 and 1910 told tales of fabulous fortunes to be made in this kind of work. As most of the activity at the parks and resorts took

place after dark, it was only with the newly available electric lights that the photographer was able to function at all. The key to resort photographers' success seems to have been the elaborate backdrops that set their subjects against another more exotic world.

J. B. Schriever's *Library of Practical Photography*, which appeared in 1909, advised:

The backgrounds should be suitable to the location of the gallery. A pier or beach scene for a seaside resort; a mountain or waterfall background for the mountains; a chute-the-chutes for an amusement park; and so on. It would be absurd to place your customers before a background of waves and beach if the gallery is situated in the mountains.

This wisdom notwithstanding, it is difficult not to admire the pluck of the Iowa photographer who installed the gigantic replica of the Niagara Falls rapids in his Des Moines studio (p. 14). The handbook quoted above further reported that "a line of comic backgrounds, to be placed in front of, and showing only the head of, the customer, with some absurd drawing for the body, are often profitable in a well-frequented resort."

Most photographers maintained a steadier and more serious studio business in the center of town, where they made portraits against plain backdrops and sold their own postcards depicting local views. When anything out of the ordinary occurred—a fire, a flood, the visit of the circus or a politician—the local cameraman was on hand, and, during the years just before the war, his pictures were likely to be produced as postcards.

Although the larger newspapers printed photographs of significant events and personalities—often as a separate gravure section in the Sunday edition—most small newspapers limited themselves to the written news, illustrated with line engravings if they could be had, until well into the 1920s. Therefore, photographs of news events had to be made available by other means, and the photographic postcard was frequently the medium chosen. Local newspaper reports of the severe hail storm in Ostrander, Minnesota, in 1908 included no pictures of the hail or the damage it did, but an enterprising photographer from a nearby town covered the disaster and quickly made up postcards for sale (p. 158).

Because postcards were made specifically to be sold, mailed, and sent with a message, the senders' comments have been reproduced in this book along with the pictures. Often written by the people pictured, or by close friends, the messages offer a rare personal commentary on the events illustrated. At a time when cars and telephones were just beginning to bring people within easy reach of each other, these postcards conveyed the small news and short messages of friendship. They showed grandparents what grandchildren wore in the Fourth of July parade. They showed a man's workplace and his tools, or the destruction caused by the spring flood. Sometimes they reminded a girl across town of a Sunday afternoon picnic. Together, they offer us an intimate view of American life some seventy years ago.

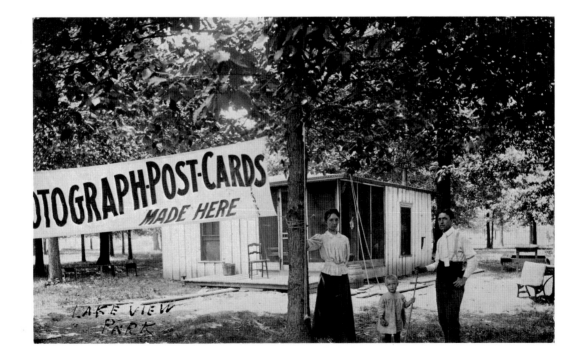

PRAIRIE FIRES
AND
PAPER MOONS

A NOTE ON THE CAPTIONS:
The messages and postmarks from the postcard
backs have been set in italic type. The imprint of the
photographer, where it was stamped or embossed on
the postcards, has been set in capital letters. The authors' notes and supplementary dating have been set
in roman type. Approximate dates have been given
where the style of the postcard back could be used to
place the date within a three-year period.

In the Photographer's Studio

AT THE HEIGHT OF THE POSTCARD CRAZE, the mails were inundated with photographs of children, suitors, and faraway friends. Many of these images were made in the controlled surroundings of a photographer's studio, where people went to record every sort of change in status and simply when the urge struck to have a portrait made. These cards document marriages, the birth of children, new suits, and even the tenure of a favorite pet.

Not long before these pictures were taken, the invention of a new and faster photographic emulsion had done away with the need for the stiff, formal poses that were the hallmark of nineteenth-century photographs. With the advent of the new, quicker exposures, the old photo-studio neck braces were retired, and people relaxed before the camera's gaze: heads tilt naturally, hands loosely hold cigars, and even an occasional smile appears.

At carnivals and amusement parks, the new stop-action photographs then being taken in the world outside were imitated in wild and fantastic studio props of rushing speedboats, swirling river rapids, and mock-up aeroplanes. Great pains were taken by the showmen-photographers to create popular and dazzling settings; the 1910 passing of Halley's Comet prompted a brief flurry of comet backdrops, and the paper moon became a widespread studio fixture—perhaps inspired by such popular songs as "Moonbeams" (1906), "Shine on Harvest Moon" (1908), and "By the Light of the Silvery Moon" (1909).

Dearest Lizzie,
This is a photo of my uncle, Hubbert Doud. And what do you think of the large BB flat Bass Horn! Everyone says he certainly can handle it. That is Gladys Herbst in Horn. She is four years old. Her father runs a picture gallery & moving picture show. She is very fond of uncle. Love, From Gertrude. 10. 10. 10

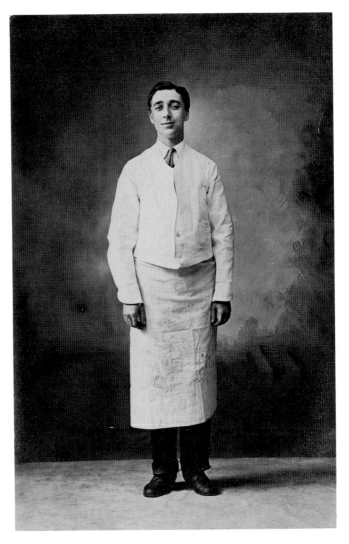

Anna & Ada Allen. Graham Sta., W. Va. Age 9 years.

About 1908.

5 Spuds 22½ lbs.

I arrived and am working today Hope to hear from you
soon I remain ever your Bro F. L. M.
About 1910.

Here's smiling at you—sincerely Will.
Twin Falls, Idaho; Nov. 25, 1907

Mr. & Mrs. Geo H Roge . . . n their honey moon. Catalina. 1911.
THE BAKER PHOTOGRAPHIC CO., AVALON, CAL.

AUDITORIUM STUDIO, ON THE
PIER, LONG BEACH, CAL.

COPE BROS, 211 FIFTH AVENUE,
CLINTON, IOWA

About 1909.

About 1907.

With best wishes From Albert.
BLANCHARD'S STUDIO, 150 MARKET ST. LYNN, MASS.
About 1910.

BODZIAK STUDIOS, 3134 RICH-
MOND ST., 4449 E. THOMPSON
ST., PHILADELPHIA, PA.

Dear Sam,
20 Sept. '10 . . . I am still on the
P. R. R. and still have the same
old game at home you know
what. I suppose you are keeping
steady and preparing for the big
day. I remain, Your old pal
Jack Bill.
HIPPODROME STUDIO, 221 5TH
AVE., PITTSBURGH, PA.

17

About 1910.

About 1910.

If you were there I could look more pleasant.

Dear Friend Myrtle,
Hope these few lines will find you feeling better.
Mrs. Howard Slemmons.
This is Busters picture—the only Card I had on hand.
Creston, Ohio; March 23, 1914.

At Home and at Play

THE AVERAGE MIDDLE-CLASS HOME in the early years of the century was a closed-in place, crowded with dark wooden furniture, hung with heavy draperies, and choking with bric-a-brac. Most family activity centered around the kitchen, where food was prepared, clothes laundered, and baths taken. This was where supplies were laid in for the winter and, in many homes, where meals were eaten. The better furniture and more elaborate decorations were reserved for the parlor, where the piano stood, if the family could afford one. The parlor may have been the least used room in the house, but it was certainly the most frequently photographed. It was the showpiece of the home, where guests were taken on Sundays and where the family posed for photographs to send to relatives.

Because flash photography was a risky business involving flaming powder and clouds of smoke, indoor pictures required a skillful camera-man—one who knew how to expose for the low levels of light that the windows admitted or one who was not afraid of the volatile flash powder. Not surprisingly, many family photographs were taken out of doors, often with parlor furnishings awkwardly displayed on a porch or lawn.

These are pictures of relaxed people enjoying themselves in familiar surroundings. They deliver a privileged view of the past—a candid glimpse of ordinary afternoons long ago.

About 1907.

Lizzie Brown.

About 1909.

PHOTO BY L. A. JOHNSON, ELMIRA, N.Y.

27

Christmas 1906.
What we found in our stockings
Chas & Hattie.

Elizabeth & her Christmas Tree.

SUNDAY JULY 23
1911. H.S.F.

Dearest Mary,
. . . This is a picture of four of my kiddies who dramatized the old story of *The Three Bears* for an entertainment. I wish you might see them. They are darlings. Grandfather talks some of going E. this summer and tho I get quite thrilled don't know if it will happen. I am crazy to see you all again. Do write soon. Heaps of love. Ellen.
St. Paul, Minn.; April 21, 1913.

Arvada, Colo.; Dec. 12, 1913.

Just a smile, I reconed that it would be as hot anywhere as in St. Louis—so, not being particular just when my name appeared in the society column I stayed at home and made a snowman last Feb. Yours, Lumys.
St. Louis, Mo.; Aug. 25, 1914.

About 1910.

Dear Friend,
. . . can you find me on this card.
your friend Emma Brandhoufer.
the woman with the cross on.
Mrs. B.

South Toe Singing Contest. Aug. 2, 1914.
Yancey County, North Carolina.

My dear Mrs. Steyers,
I wish you the happiest kind of a birthday & many more
of them. With very much love. R. S. Shaller.
Bethlehem, Pa.; April 1, 1912.

About 1909.

38

Dear Jessie Friend & Schoolmate,
I just received Bells second letter since you were hurt with my own worry and troubles I did not stop to realize you were so bad although I often think of you and wonder how you are. Away out here away from all my dear old schoolmates and friends my mind always wanders to some dear old friend for new friends are not like our dear friends of childhood days although some new friends are very dear. I often think of the big times we had playing in the snow never seeming to tire or get cold now I just hate for it to snow it seems so dreary and I don't like to wade in the snow anymore. it looks quite rainy out tonight. Hoping you will soon be well enough to come and see us. your old Friend Jane.
this is my husbands uncles house.
About 1910.

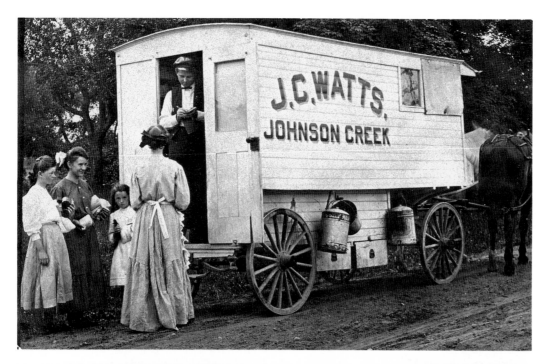

Middleport, N.Y.; July 27, 1906.

About 1909.

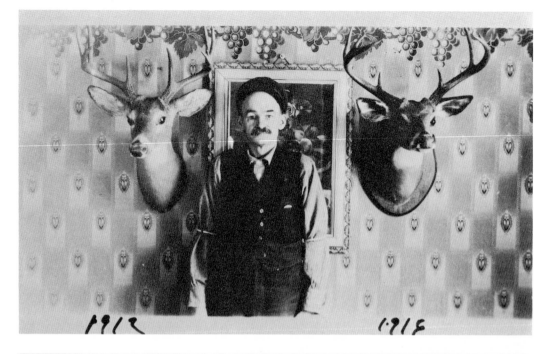

1912   1918

Friend Carl,
As you don't come over I will
send you this. I am worse with
rhumtism than I was. I got a
nice Buck this fall trip. When I
see you will tell you about the
trip. Your friend
the Buck Killer.

About 1909.

About 1909.

About 1909.

GAY'S LION FARM
EL MONTE, CALIFORNIA

45

Sand-sculpture concessions were popular at several of the country's great beaches during the early years of the century. This piece was molded by James J. Taylor of Atlantic City, who dressed for work in a dark business suit and a derby hat. The sand sculptors developed two distinct styles: quick sketches of passing bathers and extravagant showpieces that might take days or even weeks to perfect. "Cast up by the Sea," made in 1906, seems fairly natural in its construction, but later sculptors applied color, and on occasion cement, to their creations.

CANADICE LAKE

48

About 1906.

July 20, 1910.

At Work

TAKEN IN THE TIME OF TRANSITION from an agricultural to an industrial economy, these pictures show both plowed fields and the factories and mills that were reshaping the landscape—and the American way of life. Small-town photographers took the pictures they were hired to take and incidentally produced a documentary overview of the working world around them.

This was a time of expansion and progress, a time of anticipating new technologies and better working conditions. Pictured here are telephone operators and installers drawing isolated farms and towns into a vast system of instant communication, sign painters creating huge advertisements for some of the first nationally distributed products, and strikers battling for shorter hours and higher wages. Alongside these workers—and just as proud of their jobs—are the icemen, barrel makers, and wheelwrights whose work would soon be phased out by changes already in the wind.

This was a time of craft traditions carried tenuously forward into the machine age. Regardless of whether their occupations were to survive or not, the workers shown here project a sense of pride in their jobs and in the industrial progress that surrounded them.

You did not answer that letter I sent. F. M.
Goshen, Ind.; Nov. 15, 1907.

About 1910.

About 1913.

About 1908.

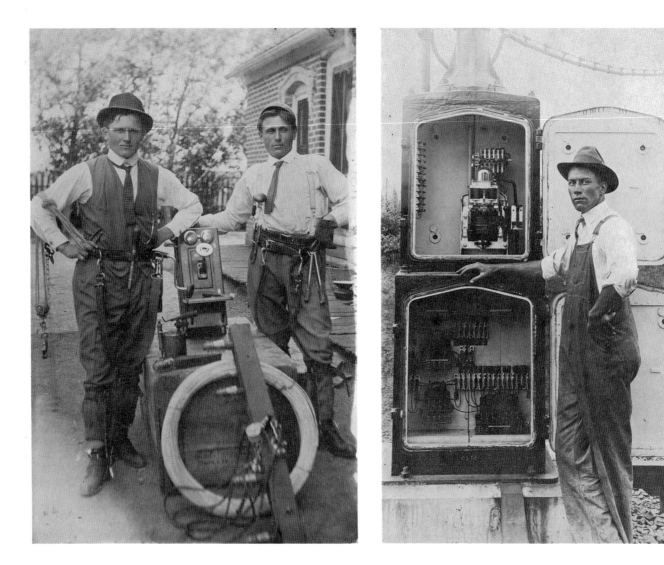

About 1911.

About 1908.

About 1909.

Dear Friend Fred,
Your are 3 months behind in
your dues let me hear from you
soon send 1 -2 or 3. Yours
Brownell.
Galeton, Pa.; June 29, 1914.

Hellow alice,
How are you I am geting along
Prety good say have you People
got very much snow out there
we ain't got very much of it
now But one Week after new
years we had about 2½ feet
and we had a very cold weather
over here too and Johns wife is
sick in Bed I Dont think she
could Live much Longer so
what is new over there answer
soon Mike Torowisky.
Steubenville, Ohio; Jan. 18,
1910.

IN MEMORY OF

IDA BRAYMAN

17 YEARS OLD

who was shot & killed by an Employer
Feb. 5th 1913 during the great struggle
of the Garment Workers of Rochester.

ISSUED BY AUTHORITY OF
UNITED GARMENT
WORKERS AMERICA
REGISTERED UNION MADE
60

Copyrigted 1913 by U. G. W. Local 14 Rochester N. Y.

Ida Braeman (as her name was spelled in the newspaper accounts) was shot in the chest while demonstrating with a group of strikers, most of them young women, in front of a tailor shop that was ignoring the garment workers' action. Miss Braeman had planned to celebrate the announcement of her engagement that evening, and her father had made the trip from New York City for the occasion.

The strikers were demanding an eight-hour day, a ten-percent wage increase, union recognition, and extra pay for overtime and holidays. When an agreement was reached in May 1913 its terms included a fifty-two-hour work week at the old fifty-four-hour rate, time and a half for overtime, no work on five legal holidays, and no reprisals for strike activity or union membership.

Lettie:
Fory wanted me to send all of
his sisters and brothers one of
these cards so I am writting
them to night. . . . and Lettie
tell me how many pennies I
owe you for the poker. Eva.
Deerfield, Ma.; Sept. 17, 1912.

MAKING ICE AT DUBOIS NEBR.

Dearest Aunt & Uncle,
If I'm not badly mistaken you
owe me a letter. Lillah.
DuBois, Neb.; Oct. 6, 1910.

Freds. Lester Lilas main cook seated. about 1911.

Dear Friend Lute,
Hope you got home all right
how would you like a pice of
this cheese? I am quite bussy
triming apples trees today. you
friend, Herm.
Mannsville, N.Y.; Mar. 20,
1909.

MAKING ITALIAN CHEESE
JEFF CO CREAMERY
ELLISBURG N Y NO 24

Dear Mrs. Reese,
I will send you a picture of the
logs above the mill at Loleta.
My husband and son are in the
picture. Mr. Gibson is the 3rd
from left side Harris our son is
4th from the right. Give my
best regards to your mother and
Mr. Reese and thanking you for
the kindness shown us while in
your home. Your friend
Mrs. H. A. Gibson.
About 1910.

About 1913.

A.W. ERICSON PHOTO, ARCATA, CAL'A

Prescott, Wash.; April 10, 1912.

Ed Whitehead, John R.

Dear Alice,
This is a sample of our busy cotton season: The Frisco Depot platform. I have marked Perry and David. Hope you are all well. Helen.
Van Buren, Ark.; Nov. 6, 1908.

About 1909.

70

About 1912.

Mr. Arthur Mitchell, Omaha, Neb.; July 24, 1918.

Dear Heinie,
Just a line to let you know I haven't forgotten you. Am on the road for fair now. Working for the Jello concern now. Just came back from the mountains and start for Sonora in the morning. We have to get every town in Calif. Will write later.
Your old friend (tough Guy)
Tom Reardon.
Farmington, Ca; Sept. 11, 1919.
BRANNON'S STUDIO, 625 E.
MAIN ST., STOCKTON.

W. F. CHAMP

W. J. WYNN

Sherburne Electric Light Station, Sherburne, N.Y.

About 1909.

FUNERAL PROCESSION, MINE DISASTER VICTIMS, SYKESVILLE, PA. JULY 18, 1911

The Cascade Mines in Sykesville, Pennsylvania suffered two disasters in the summer of 1911. The first, in June, killed eleven coal miners; the second, in July, killed twenty-one.

IVAN RAWSON, PHOTOGRA-
PHER, RICHMOND, MASS.
About 1910.

Beaumont, Texas; Nov. 26,
1912.

CUPEL BOTTOM, $125,000 IN CRUDE GOLD
HOMESTAKE MINING CO., LEAD, S.D.
PHOTO BY LEASE

About 1910.

About 1910.

About 1910.

Perhaps you don't recognize the subject. When school begins I will have time to make those other pictures.
Fort Smith, Ark.; Sept. 8, 1908.

Mamma says I look as though I had a board strapped on my back. Beginning at the left they are: Mrs. Minnie Vine, Addie Ford, Hazel Van Arsdalen, Mrs. Anna Hicker, Mr. Van Arsdalen the Proprietor and little I _____? Bessie Emerick and Ivah Van Arsdalen at the right. About 1908.

You Are Cordially Invited to Honor us with a Visit of Inspection. A Large and Varied Selection in Spring Millinery will be on Display at our Opening Friday and Saturday Mar. 31–Apr. 1. Style, Quality, and Workmanship in Every Hat and Prices Reasonable. Come and See. You Will Be Heartily Welcome Whether You Buy or Not. The Elliots.
LeRoy, Mich.; March 29, 1911.

Addison, Michigan.

OSBORN, PHOTOGRAPHER,
WITH G&K DRUG CO.,
RAWHIDE, NEV.

About 1909.

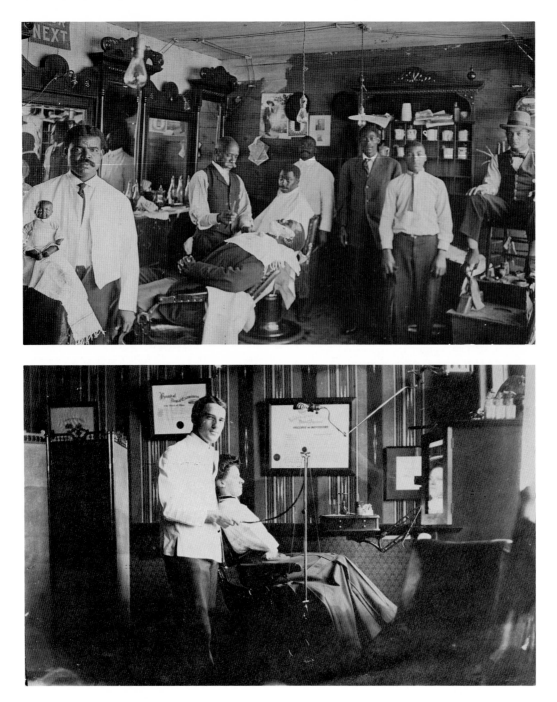

Dr. L. E. Howk & Miss Bessie Smith.
About 1907.

About 1909.

Feb. 21, 1911. Photographed in Independent Office, Coffeyville, Kan. Jan. 1911. Rather late for a valentine, but better late than never. Come over and watch me work the keys. Lovingly, Flo.

Greetings from M. Roke.
W. H. CUBBERLY, 1332 WALNUT ST., CINCINNATI, OHIO.
COMMERCIAL AND HOME PORTRAIT PHOTOGRAPHER
About 1910.

Eden, N.Y. George Pyrits,
Olympic Runner. Photo taken
in father's Drug Store.
About 1913.

Mrs. Lora B. Bryant and sister, Mrs. Happa A. Latty, folding and boxing GRACE - MAE HOSIERY. During their fifty four years of service in this mill, they have boxed and folded 71, 280, 000 pairs of stockings.

BOVEE'S STUDIO, QUINCY, MICH.

Dear Friend Darus,
This is a view of a Silo being
moved whole, it was 12 ft. in
diameter, you can see how
large it is beside the man who
is standing on Top of Silo & the
one beside it, it was quite a
sight seeing it moved whole.
We saw it go past Evas. The
man by the horses is Ethels
Father-in-Law. Ever friend
Celia.
PHOTO POST CARD BY M.P.
CLARK, WILLIAMSBURG, MASS.
About 1910.

88

Charles W. Smiley, Grocers, 35 Crystal St., E. Stroudsburg, Pa.
About 1914.

Dear Cousin,
This Photo is a 7 ton gear wheel 10' 2" diameter which it took 6 teams to haul up the Slate
Run mountain, this machinery we put in a year ago last fall the wheel goes on one of our oil
Pumps. J. B. Tomb.
About 1908.

At War

IN 1917, THE UNITED STATES joined the Great War in Europe "to make the world safe for democracy." Thousands of young men were pulled into the conflict; from cities, small towns, and rural areas they were shipped overseas to confront the horrors of modern warfare. Poison gas, armored tanks, flame throwers, and long-range guns made the war a waking nightmare for the ordinary foot soldier.

But there were glamour and excitement to be had as well. The armed services took many soldiers away from their small communities for the first time; together they met other soldiers from all across the United States and discovered the great cities of Europe.

The war also marked the end of an era in American life; when the soldiers returned home in 1918 and 1919, many found their small towns limiting and old fashioned. "How ya gonna keep 'em down on the farm after they've seen Paree?" went the words to a popular song, and, indeed, many veterans left their hometowns for the glitter of the cities.

World War I, as we now call it, was a brutal experience. This epic global conflict left millions dead or maimed and caused immeasurable social upheaval. It is sad to realize that some of the very photographs reproduced here must have been mementos of sons and lovers who never returned.

This is buck and is friend and we was lucke we got them
it was 6 o clock I will send you my picture in a nother.
This is for Nays and dont be mad and show it to my
friends and dont forget to show fisher and the Strong
man.

FALKER'S STUDIO, EASTON, PA.

Hello Mr. Leslie,
How are you Fine I hope This is
a part of the mess coock I am in
the Rear With Love Leo
U.S.S. Louisiana; May 21, 1917
PASSED BY CENSOR

Telaphone Detail.
18th Balloon Co.
France. Dec. 2[?]

Dec. 20, 1918

HEAVY PACKED
WiTH GAS MASK

*Pvt. Philip Warren, Camp Funston, Kans., 3rd Co., 4th Bn.
From Rentiesville, Okla.*

The 92nd Division was the official black division in World War I. Authorized by the Secretary of War in May 1917, its officers were trained at Fort Des Moines, Iowa, and its headquarters were established at Camp Funston, Fort Riley, Kansas. The division went into action in the front lines in France in August 1918.

Mascot. Leslie Walker of 3rd Co., 4th Bn., 164 D.B.,
Camp Funston, Kans., From Kans. City, Mo., In service
fourteen months.

Pvt. Willie Hickman, Texas.

Patrick J. Canfield. Somewhere in France.

Bro Dan From Edwin.

*New York City in Wild Celebration as Germany Signs
Armistice.* © *I. E. S. From N. Moser, N.Y.*

To Sister Emma From Wes and Hattie 1918. taken in front of the Hotel.

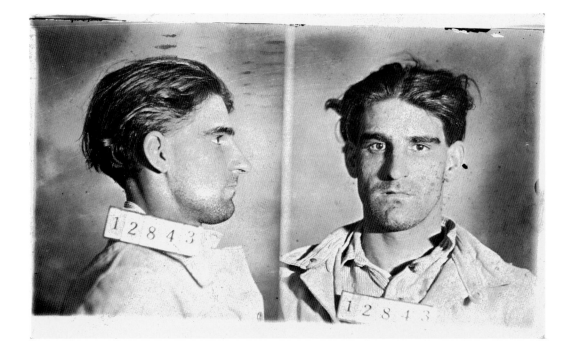

Outside the Law

THESE FEW IMAGES relating to crime and criminals are among the rarest photographic postcards. Some were sent to police chiefs to aid in the capture of lawbreakers, and some must have been kept on file by prison wardens in the event of escapes. The more sensational photographs, of course, were made for sale by local photographers hoping to cash in on the flurry of interest that surrounded the capture or hanging of a noted outlaw. Since photographs were rarely printed along with the newspaper accounts that documented these events, the postcards may have been the only images available to the public. A number of these cards seem to have been purchased and saved as souvenirs, with a few key facts scribbled on the backs for memory's sake.

Ranging from pictures of Black Handers—as mafiosi were then called—to confiscated whiskey stills and a western train robber, the cards give us an idea of the crimes that caught the public eye. These were the last days of the old-fashioned outlaws of the West and the formative years for organized crime in the cities. Prohibition, the widespread use of the automobile, and better road surfaces combined after 1920 to mobilize and strengthen the criminal element.

Left his home in Ilion, N. Y., February 19, 1912

WALTER A. STEVENS

Walter A. Stevens, white, 37 years old, height 5 feet 6 inches, 145 pounds, slender built, medium complexion, black hair with slight curl on left side, high forhead, brown eyes, small mustache, sometimes smooth face. Upper lip slightly projecting, wears a dark brown suit, soft brown hat, brown derby or straw sailor hat, also wears dark blue suit, black laced shoes or Oxford ties, soft shirt, four-in-hand tie with opal pin or stiff bosom white shirt with opal stud. Gold watch with monogram "W. A. S." inside of case, double gold chain, seal charm, silver match safe with "W. A. S" attached to one end of the chain. Gold ring with green stone, laundry has initials "W. A. S. and No. 9730.' Member of Ilion Lodge, No. 400, I. O. O. F., also F. C. Warner Camp, No. 52, Spanish War Veterans. Mr. Stevens is of good habits and there is no reason to account for his disappearance. Will you please have inquiries made of all automobile, typewriter and gun shops, also in all auto garages—as he is a good mechanic, and telegraph any imformation to Mrs. W. A. Stevens, or Wm. H. Stitt, Chief of Police, at Ilion, N. Y.

The Dalles, Oregon, Nov. 4, 1914.
Dear Sir:

HARUGI KISHI, Japanese, wanted for jumping his bills. Above is a good picture of him. Description: Age 32. Height 5 feet 4 inches. Weight 125. Eyes black. Slim built. Smooth shaven, but has heavy stand of beard. Drinks some and gambles. Barber by profession, but will work at anything. If apprehended, please arrest and wire me.

E. KURTZ, Chief of Police.

1905 Police Car Taking in C.H.Rogers
for murders.

Officers Arrive at Olney Farm with C.H.Rogers.

Tripple murder of the Olney family near
Middletown N.Y.

In May 1907, Charles Henry Rogers was apprehended in California and brought to New York by train as a suspect in the mysterious Olney farm murder of 1905. On the train he confessed the crime and described in detail shooting the two elderly Olney brothers and fatally clubbing nine-year-old Alice Ingerick, their housekeeper's daughter.

Rogers told the officers on the train that he had planned the murders for a month because he believed the Olneys had a large amount of money hidden in the house and on their persons. He said, however, that after the killings he was only able to find about $70. In October 1907 Rogers was convicted of murder in the first degree for killing Fred R. Olney.

WEST VIRGINIA STATE POLICE WITH CONFISCATED STILLS, WHITESVILLE W. VA.

Whitesville, W. Va.

J. A. Landis and his blood-hounds were brought to Grantsville, Maryland to find the thieves who had dynamited the safe at the Broadwater store. On the first day the dogs led police to the home of a Mr. Proudfoot who made a partial confession to the crime. The trail then led into Pennsylvania and to the homes of two accomplices. Before returning home, Mr. Landis also tracked down a turkey thief in Pennsylvania.

Elmer McCurdy, alias Curtis, was suspected of leading a gang that robbed the mail train of the M K & T railroad on October 5, 1911. Rewards totaling $2,000 were offered by several railroad companies for McCurdy's capture. One Sheriff Freas of Pawhuska, Oklahoma, led the search that located McCurdy at an abandoned farm in the Osage hills—long a refuge for bandits and outlaws. McCurdy refused to surrender, and after a half-hour gun battle was found dead in the hay shed where he was hiding. His body was brought into Pawhuska where it was identified by railroad detectives and a Post Office inspector and viewed by a number of towns-people.

Thanks for your card. Sorry I didn't get to see you while here
But Suppose the 10 min was long enough as you dont like Fairmont.
Fairmont, W. Va.; Apr. 16, 1909.

The Hanging of "Black Jack" the Outlaw.

Local Scenes and Events

MILLIONS OF COLOR POSTCARDS of cities and major tourist attractions were printed by commercial publishers, but small-town views and pictures of the events of rural life survive primarily on the scarcer photographic postcards made by local cameramen. Working on commission or on speculation, the small-town photographers took pictures of almost every public occurrence around them. Some of these postcards may be the only photographs that exist of certain small towns and remote villages.

What is most wonderful about these postcards is their emphasis on the minor events in out-of-the-way places. They show walkers on route from Indiana to San Francisco, hopeful of setting a speed record or winning a purse from the local walkers' club. They show a round barn under construction in western Ohio and an aeroplane builder in Iowa—subjects fascinating now, but probably not even mentioned in the local newspapers of the day.

Taken together, these pictures give us insight into the fabric of small-town life in the first years of the century—the places and personalities that made up the everyday scene and the events that gave it variety.

From Mrs. Laura Selby.
About 1909.

About 1909.

*I have got a very mean place to work. They have got the
station all cut up in Rooms. C. Parrow.
Hammond, N.Y.; Oct. 22, 1908.*

PRETER BROS. FAMOUS POST
CARDS. MADE AT BRIDGE-
PORT, O.
About 1908.

Lenita Potter and Joe Rolio.
About 1908.

Mom,
This is a picture of a chair in
which the only President (Taft)
of the U. S. ever sat to look at a
moving picture show. W. H. L.
Washington, D.C.; Aug. 5,
1909.

Between 1903 and 1920, Billy Sunday led a surge of evangelistic fervor that tied in closely with the movement for prohibition. The evangelist ministers were hired by the churches in a city to conduct a four- to twelve-week campaign, during which the churches would refrain from holding regular services and for which a "tabernacle" would be built to seat the thousands of combined parishioners. The evangelists, for their part, won the public back to the church, railed against the vices of gambling and drink, and raised needed funds. After successful campaigns, newly righteous townspeople acted swiftly to close local saloons and gambling houses. During a ten-week campaign in New York City in 1917, Billy Sunday amassed 98,000 converts and raised $120,000.

Dr. Stough was somewhat less successful in his efforts. He led many poorly attended campaigns and suffered frequent setbacks as the result of his fiery temper and lack of political finesse. In June 1915, he became the defendant in a libel suit in Hazelton, Pennsylvania, after denouncing an alderman, a liquor dealer, and two city officials as "riff raff" and "plug uglies."

Tracy & Pierre, R. P. O.; Nov. 12, 1907.

Our First School In Stanley C O. S D.

Dear friend Geo.,
Thats the way we get Pabst
Beer known in Newark, N.J.
Newark, N.J.; March 24, 1908.

Dear Friend,
I thought I would drop you a
post card and let you know I
am still alive, but will write
later I guess you can tell by this
picture what I am doing . . . I
remain, John.
San Antonio, Texas; March 24,
1917.

On February 19, 1907, Passenger Car No. 1 of the Kingston Consolidated Railroad ran off its track and into the slip of the old Newark Lime and Cement Company. Conductor Walter Flannery and motorman Richard Hauser were in charge of the car and six passengers were aboard. One of the passengers, reached in his hospital bedroom, recalled thinking before the accident that the car was traveling unnecessarily fast.

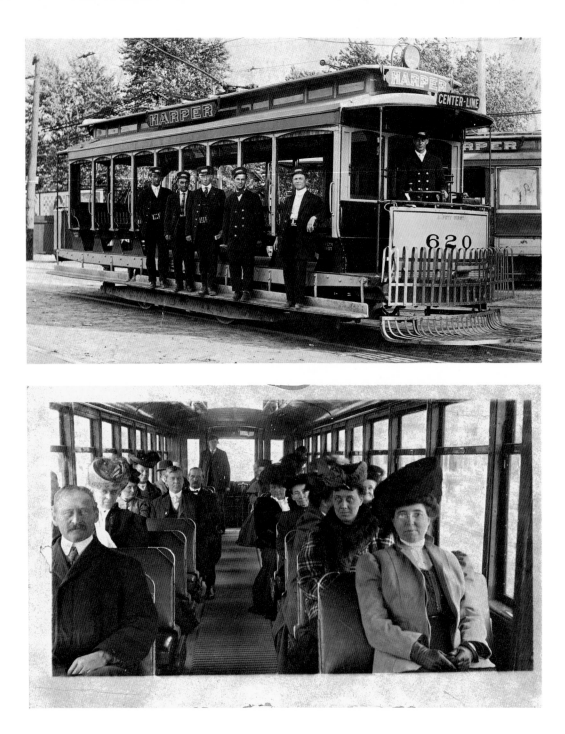

This fellow at the left is no friend of mine but he was bound to be in the picture. I would like very much to have had my mo-torman with me. Now when you have one of yourself and your better half just send me down one.

About 1908.

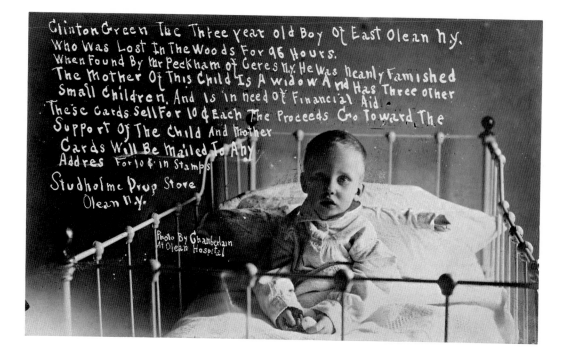

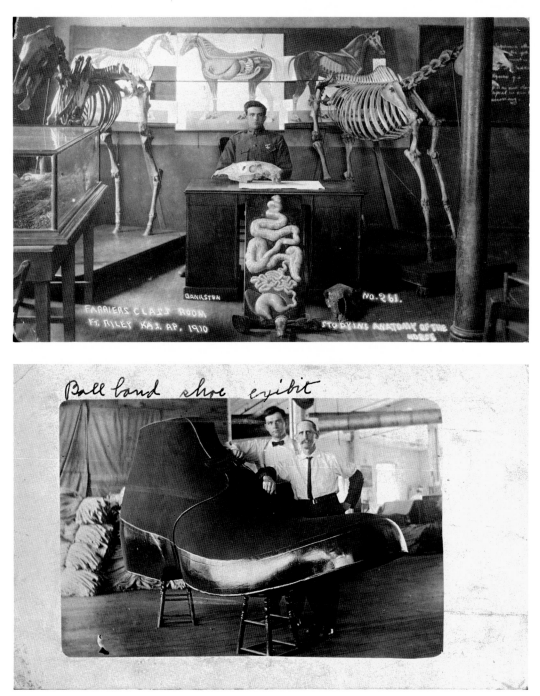

A few of the easiest things wee have too study. this is a chum of Mine in the class room. George.

Dear Beryl, I am in mishawaka like it Averil. kiss baby for me. Mishawaka, Ind.; Aug. 12, 1909.

Hello Walt:
How is this for one day's hunt. He is a friend of mine. The lion
in the middle was 9 ft. 8 in. from tip to tip. Will write soon.
Harry.
Eureka, Montana; Mar. 11, 1908.

How would you like to side step rattlesnakes? Thats what this country is noted for. I have a case here, it is over 200 miles west of Aberdeen. Weather fine. Thursday. W. F. C. About 1913.

Dear F.,
I & Ruby & Baby are well and hope you are the same. Thought you would come down this Xmas. I wish you a Merry Christmas and a happy new year. We haven't any snow yet, been the finest weather I ever saw. Elmer Draper.
Pearl, Ill.; Dec. 22, 1910.

"THE FUR MAN" J. B. Treister

Dear Sir,
I beg to inform you that I will call on you Thursday April
8th with Jackman's Fur line. Yours, J. B. Treister.
Rome, N.Y.; April 5, 1909.

Pvts. James Baggs—Fla. & Fred Horrice—Ga.

Feb 27, 1918

ED WARD + WIFE WALKING 27,000
MILES IN 3 YEARS AND 6 MONTHS.

PHOTOGRAPHER, C. G. SMITH, SEA SIDE DRUG STORE,
DAYTONA BEACH, FLA.

The sport of competitive walking thrived from the 1860s
to the 1920s. Week-long walking contests were held in
New York's Madison Square Garden, and large purses
were offered in walking races between cities.

Elmer Harkins set out for San Francisco from Alliance, Ohio, pulling a cart in which he stored extra clothes and travel necessities. In a suitcase he carried religious "mottoes," posters, and other novelties that he offered for sale along the way.

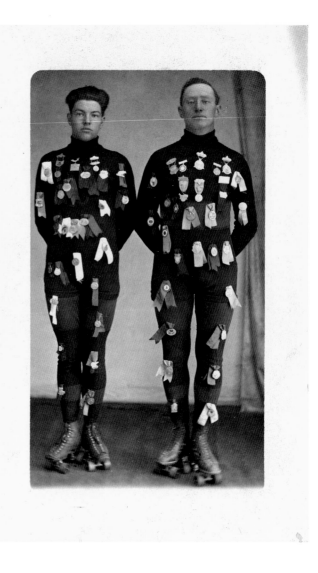

AMERICAN PHOTO GALLERY, 200 E. WALNUT ST., DES MOINES, IOWA.

AMERICANS AND INSURECTOS AT RIO GRANDE

Well Lillie,
how are you by this time hope well are you ready to come out
Pretty Soon I guess its time for you and John to come and I am
glad to if you come once but its Pretty hot Just now out here I
think you was glad that you was home over the battle from
Cracker Jack S. Weaver.

The "insurrectos" pictured here are probably soldiers under the command of Pancho Villa. During the early years of the Mexican Revolution—between 1910 and 1914—Villa skillfully led the northern arm of the struggle against the Huerta government. At this time Villa's troops maintained cordial relations with their American neighbors; the revolutionaries regularly herded stolen cattle over the border into Texas in return for guns and ammunition. After Huerta's defeat, however, the several factions of the revolution were unable to form a cohesive alliance, and Villa resumed his military activity against his earlier compatriots and on occasion against the United States. In 1916 he led his forces on a raid into the border town of Columbus, New Mexico, attacking the camp of the 13th U. S. Cavalry and making off with a cache of weapons. This led to the fruitless Punitive Expedition, headed by General John J. (Black Jack) Pershing, which marched into Mexico, but was unable to capture Villa.

Crossing the Missouri Near Williston. N.D.

Williston, N. D.; June 2, 1912

#31 COW BOYS "BEDROOM."

Hello Dad,
This is the Kind of beds they
have out here. The horses are in
a correll back of the chuck
wagon, but do not show up in
the picture. We had a fine rain
here yesterday and everything
is o.k. Ed.
Bovina, Texas; July 8, 1911.

About 1908.

144

SWAN'S STUDIO, GROVE CITY, MINN.

Henry Clay, Hamilton, Ind.

My dear Lil,
here we are waiting for you & Mr. Andrus. Doesn't this pop-
corn wagon make you homesick? We aren't going to take any
trips until you come. The weather is fine & we are enjoying a
nice quiet rest. Julia too is anxiously awaiting you. Love Els.
So hurry up.
Petuskev, Mich.; July 22, 1914.

Gene McInturff   Hutchinson, Ks

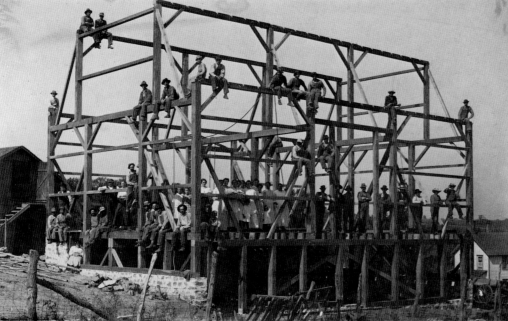

Dear ruby,
How are you by this time I am
fine and hope you are the same
I go home alright tell Dewey
don't for get about Saturday
night See if you find my picture
on this card. From
XXXXOOOXXXXXXXX G. S.
Winslow, Ill.; Oct. 9, 1914.

Horace Greeley Duncan, of Knightstown, Indiana, built round barns from about 1905 to 1915, mostly in Indiana, although this one was in Ohio. One Duncan barn still stands in Effingham, Illinois.

Harry Chaplin standing next to the smoke stack.

GRIFFITH'S STUDIO, 2602 WASHINGTON AVE., NEWPORT NEWS, VA.

Hello Maurice,
This is the Gang I work in. See if you can find me.
McComb, Ohio; April 19, 1909.

WATER TANK
CHISHOLM.

The Water Tank Going Down.
May.7.'09   "Copyrighted" by
W.H.Lawton.
Vermillion. S.D.

About 1910.

WRECK ON L.S. & M.S. WAUSEON O. — CRON.

About 1909.

HOFFMAN THRESHING RIG — MARKHAM BRIDGE — LESUEUR RIVER, MINNESOTA

C.V.R.R. Montpelier Jct. 27.

TORNADO-LONEROCK-WIS MAY 21-18
McKillop & RUUD
Photo #10

On April 12, 1911, this tornado leveled the village of Big Heart, Oklahoma. Five people were killed and about fifty others were injured. Property losses were estimated at $100,000.

To My Dear Sis,
This looks just like the cloud was before she commenced turning oh sis you can never imagine what it is like.
By By Dollie.
Omaha, Neb; Apr. 6, 1913.

The March 23, 1913, Omaha tornado was the most destructive storm ever to hit that area of the country. It struck at 6:00 PM on Easter Sunday and in just twelve minutes carved a swath a quarter mile wide and five miles long through the center of the city.

Hail Stones Gathered at Ostrander, Minn. Twenty Four Hours After The Hail Storm Of June 20 1908 Weight of Largest ¼ lb.

Photo By Harden Le Roy, Minn

The Ostrander, Minnesota, hail storm lasted less than an hour, but left the region devastated. The hail stripped trees of their leaves and bark, pounded crops into the ground, smashed windows, and punched holes in the roofs of houses and barns. Furniture and pianos in many houses were totally destroyed by hail coming through shattered windows. Hail stones three inches in diameter were picked up after the storm, and in places the ice was piled three and four feet high.

Many thanks call again Mrs. Surface Three River Michigan.

Great Barn Fire
Briarcliff NY Apl 28 1913

A MIDNIGHT VIEW OF THE TRIPP CO. PRAIRIE FIRE.
DALLAS. S.D.   COPYRIGHT BY S. DOWNEY.

My dear Louise,
I wish you would hunt up my
bath-robe and bath slippers
and send them to me. They are
in the attic. Tom.
Dallas, S. Dakota; May 15,
1909.

This is a photo of an oil tank (25,000 barrels) struck by light-
ning. I saw this fire. "Edward." How is Effie? Give my regards
to her and your mother and sister. Ed.

Gala Occasions

IN THIS ERA OF TELEVISION, it is hard to imagine the excitement the traveling circus once held for Americans. It brought a taste of the exotic to what were still largely isolated communities. With it came freaks and fat ladies, acrobats from Europe, handsome ringmasters, elephants from Africa, and beautiful sirens on horseback. The circus provided a glittery escape from the cares of day-to-day life, and to people unspoiled by the constant entertainment that was to come with radio—and even more hypnotically with television—a day at the circus was a wondrous event, anticipated beforehand and cherished long afterward.

In a similar way, parades, county fairs, and traveling entertainments provided important interludes of relaxation and diversion. The Fourth of July, the major public celebration of the year in most small towns, came after all the crops had been planted and the warm weather had arrived. It gave the town a chance to create its own glamour: ordinary cars and wagons were transformed into fantasy floats for the parade, and at night the whole community came together to watch the spectacular fireworks displays. These times of celebration were the high points of the year, and, not surprisingly, were often shared with friends through photographic postcards.

About 1909.

Sept. 20, 1904.

About 1906.

167

"AKRON"

Length, 258 ft. Weight of Bag 5,000 lbs. Maximum H.P. of Engines 317 H.P.
Diameter, 47 ft. Cubic Capacity 40,000 ft. Carries 1540 Gallons gasoline.
Length of car 185 ft. Weight of car 6,000 lbs.

PHOTOGRAPHS BY ... SMITH ...

Melvin Vaniman, America's most innovative dirigible engineer, designed the *Akron* in 1911 specifically for an attempt at an Atlantic crossing. Shortly after the airship was built, Vaniman, working with engineers at the Goodyear Rubber Company, perfected a steel-wire cloth that was fifty times stronger than any fabric previously developed. Proud as he was of the discovery, Vaniman lamented to reporters that the finished *Akron* lacked the new material. "She was the latest word in ballooning last summer. And now—well she is a back number already. I am only sorry that my trip across the Atlantic has to be made in her. Because of course it has to be made." On July 2, 1912, while on a trial flight over the beach at Atlantic City, the *Akron* exploded, killing Vaniman, his brother, and the three other flight hands aboard.

Springfield Fair, Springfield, Vt., Sept. 2, '08

About 1910.

Dear Grandma,
Here is another Picture of
Anita. Sending it with much
Love. R. W. H.
Pittsburg, Kans.; July 6, 1910.

Dear Jennie,
Here you can see our Band. I
spose you can find Mr. Larsen,
it is from the 4 of July. I am sor-
row I did not send you a card
before but you will have to ex-
cuse me as I have been busy
caning fruit. Best regards to
you. From a Friend
Anna Larsen.
Kimballton, Iowa; Aug. 24,
1909.

Begun in 1874, after a spontaneous burst of zeal on the part of women across the country, the National Women's Christian Temperance Union, or W.C.T.U., swelled into a powerful force in the 1880s and kept growing through the first two decades of the century. Early in its fight for prohibition, the W.C.T.U. added the women's vote to its goals, as a means of winning temperance legislation, and thus became a progressive force in the women's movement.

I hope you are enjoying your-
selves. When you think of it
and if your funds have not run
out write and tell me how the
Isle is. Yours truly,
Frank R. Pier.
Buffalo, N.Y.; Aug. 26, 1913.

173

The Women's Political Union was founded in New York City in January 1907 on three basic principles: that working-class and professional women must both be brought into the struggle for suffrage, that propaganda must be made more dramatic, and that the organization must devote itself to political action. Harriot Blatch took charge of the union and succeeded in the next month in getting the suffrage issue debated in both houses of the New York legislature, where it was soundly defeated. By June 1908 the union had 19,000 members, and it continued its activities until 1911, when it became part of the coalition called the Women's Suffrage Party, a national organization. New York State passed a suffrage amendment in 1917, and in 1920 the federal amendment was ratified by two-thirds of the states.

H. GERLACH'S DEUTSCHER
BAZAAR, 39 ERSTE STR.,
94 RIVER ST.
This eagle rested on the prow
of the steamer *Imperator,* built
for the Hamburg American
Line in 1912. The sculpture,
cast in bronze, was the work
of Professor Bruno Kruse of
Berlin. After World War I the
Imperator was appropriated by
England; there she served the
Cunard Line under the name
Berengaria.

*Sunday School Excursion. Ed.
July 19/10.*
Lake Hopatcong, N. J.
HARRIS PHOTO POST CARD CO.,
PITTSTON, PA. AND MT. AR-
LINGTON, N.J.

Charles Wagner. Chatham Sq., Chinatown, N York.
About 1920.
Chatham Square, on the Lower East Side of New York City, was the center of the tattooist's art from the 1870s through the 1940s. Charles Wagner learned the art there from Samuel F. O'Reilly and set up his business around 1900. During the period of enlistment and draft for World War I the tattoo business thrived as never before, but fell off considerably after the armistice. Wagner stayed on in Chatham Square through the 1940s.

JOHN McLAUCHLIN,
WOODSIDE PARK,
PHILADELPHIA, PA.
The Domino House at Wood-
side Park was engineered along
the lines of Coney Island's
Crazy House. The floors
moved, the domino walls
shifted, and a trick stairway
stretched out into a ramp, top-
pling visitors and landing them
at the exit in a heap.

"Amalie" the tallest living lady in the world. Height 7ft. 2in.

JOLLY EMA ... WEIGHT 620 LBS

About 1909.

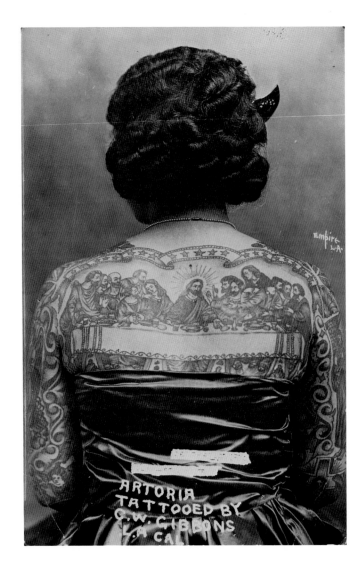

APPENDIX:

Methods of Dating Photographic Postcards

Many photographic postcards bear postmarks that accurately identify the time of their mailing, and most seem to have been mailed shortly after they were made. Cards without postmarks may be dated approximately by examining the wording and design of the printed labels on the backs. Postal regulations changed on three occasions, dictating changes in the type on the card backs, and the photographic manufacturers periodically altered the design of the printing, in some cases two or three times a year. Together, these factors allow for fairly accurate dating of most photographic postcards.

Although the earliest example of an American photographic postcard included by the authors in this survey is dated October 21, 1902, the cards were almost certainly made as early as July 1898, when the mailing of picture postcards with the label PRIVATE MAILING CARD on the back was authorized by an act of Congress. After December 24, 1901, postal regulations allowed the use of the shorter label POST CARD on the card backs. The PRIVATE MAILING CARD imprint could still be used, and occasionally was, but manufacturers and publishers seem to have preferred the shorter POST CARD, and as the postcard fad began to take hold, this imprint appeared on almost all cards.

Until 1907 the Post Office required that any messages on the cards be put on the picture side so that the address could not be obscured. These early postcards, with their backs reserved strictly for the address, are referred to as "undivided backs." Several variants of early undivided backs appear in the dating table below, but most can be approximately dated between 1904, when the sending of postcards began to be a popular pastime, and 1907, when a further relaxation of the postal law permitted messages as well as addresses on the backs of the cards.

After March 1, 1907, manufacturers began to sell photographic postcard stock with a space for correspondence marked on the back. These postcards are referred to below as "divided backs," and for more specific dating it is necessary to look carefully at the design of the type and its position.

As most postcards were made on manufactured stock, it is possible to verify the dating results in a broad way with information from the major photographic manufacturers of the period. The Eastman Kodak Company first listed a photographic postcard stock—"Velox"—in its 1902 catalogue. In 1904, the company added "Azo" and two other papers to its postcard line. "Azo" and "Velox," along with the Ansco Company's competing brand, "Cyko," were the papers most commonly used in the period covered in this book.

The dates given below for the various styles of postcard backs are based on dated and postmarked cards. To identify a particular style of card on which a postage stamp had obscured the stamp box design, strong backlighting through a stamp-sized mask was used to see through the stamp, a method similar to the "candling" of eggs. To preserve the backs of the cards, stamps were not steamed off. The following list includes the most common postcard types. A more thorough classification could isolate over one hundred brands and variations.

The concept and groundwork for this dating study were provided by the article "Dating Early Photography by Card Mounts and Other External Evidence: Tentative Suggestions," by Arnold R. Pilling (*Image* 17, NO. 1. [March 1974]).

To use this dating table, determine whether the card back is divided or undivided, and check in the stamp corner for the brand of the paper stock. Then identify by type design and placement. Only the most common postcard types have been included, and not every variation listed is illustrated.

UNDIVIDED BACKS

1. Solid CYKO symbol in stamp box, with PRINTS AT NIGHT written in tail of "C" (see ill.).

Earliest: Apr. 1905
Latest: Aug. 1906
Number in sample: 4

2. Hollow CYKO symbol in stamp box; hollow POST CARD with extended tail on "R" (see ill.).

Earliest: July 1906
Latest: Oct. 1908
Number in sample: 11

3. Same style hollow POST CARD as 2, but stamp box made up of lines of dots; no CYKO symbol.

Earliest: Aug. 1905
Latest: Aug. 1906
Number in sample: 10

4. Blue-print paper; blue type on postcard back.

Earliest: July 1906
Latest: July 1907
Number in sample: 17

5. Sailboat in circle in stamp box; thin sans-serif POST CARD (see ill.).

Earliest: Apr. 1905
Latest: Feb. 1908
Number in sample: 27

6. Hand in circle in stamp box; same POSTCARD as 5 (see ill.).

Earliest: Oct. 1905
Number in sample: 1

7. Same POST CARD as 5, but no brand symbol in stamp box.

Earliest: Jan. 1906
Latest: Apr. 1907
Number in sample: 6

8. Stamp box made up of lines of dots; POST CARD in hollow, decorative type; label THIS SIDE FOR THE ADDRESS; word "ADDRESS" ends under left side of "R" of "CARD" (see ill.).

Earliest: July 1906
Latest: Aug. 1906
Number in sample: 5

9. Same stamp box and POST CARD as 8, but word "ADDRESS" ends under right side of "R" of "CARD."

Earliest: Sept. 1906
Latest: Dec. 1906
Number in sample: 3

10. Same stamp box and POST CARD as 8, but word "ADDRESS" ends under center of "R" of "CARD."

Earliest: Aug. 1906
Latest: Oct. 1907
Number in sample: 11

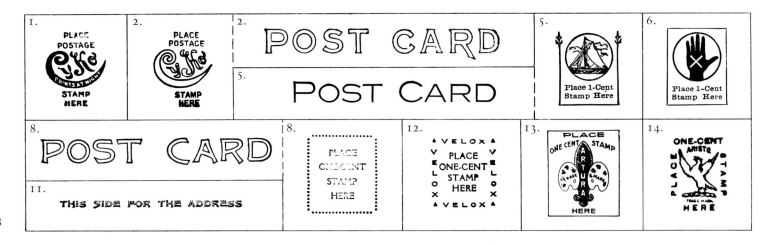

11. Same stamp box and POST CARD as 8; label, THIS SIDE FOR THE ADDRESS, in hollow type (see ill.).

Earliest: Sept. 1905
Latest: Oct. 1906
Number in sample: 8

12. Same POST CARD as 8, but with VELOX stamp box with upward-pointing triangles at corners (see ill.).

Earliest: Dec. 1906
Latest: Nov. 1908
Number in sample: 8

13. ARTURA fleur-de-lis symbol in stamp box (see ill.).

Earliest: Dec. 1906
Latest: June 1907
Number in sample: 4

14. ARISTO eagle symbol in stamp box (see ill.).

Earliest: Apr. 1906
Latest: Dec. 1906
Number in sample: 5

DIVIDED BACKS

15. AZO stamp box with diamonds in corners (see ill.); POST CARD same style as 8, labels CORRESPONDENCE HERE and NAME AND ADDRESS HERE.

Earliest: Apr. 1907
Latest: Sept. 1908
Number in sample: 27

16. AZO stamp box with upward-pointing triangles in corners (see ill.); same POST CARD as 8; labels CORRESPONDENCE HERE and NAME AND ADDRESS HERE.

Earliest: Aug. 1907
Latest: Oct. 1912
Number in sample: 109 (100 of 109 examples from 1907–9)

17. AZO stamp box with upward-pointing triangles in corners; hollow POST CARD with straight crossbar on "A" (see ill.); labels CORRESPONDENCE and ADDRESS; left side of stamp box above first "s" of "ADDRESS."

Earliest: Aug. 1909
Latest: June 1911
Number in sample: 11

18. AZO stamp box with upward-pointing triangles in corners; same POST CARD as 17; labels CORRESPONDENCE HERE and NAME AND ADDRESS HERE.

Earliest: Jan. 1910
Latest: July 1918
Number in sample: 77

19. AZO stamp box with triangles in corners (upward-pointing triangles at top, downward pointing triangles at bottom); same POST CARD as 17; labels CORRESPONDENCE and ADDRESS.

Earliest: Dec. 1918
Latest: 1930
Number in sample: 47 (41 of 47 examples from 1918–22)

20. AZO stamp box with squares in corners; same POST CARD as 17.

Earliest: 1926
Latest: 1939
Number in sample: 12

21. VELOX stamp box with diamonds in corners (see ill.); same POST CARD as 8; labels CORRESPONDENCE HERE and NAME AND ADDRESS HERE.

Earliest: Aug. 1907
Latest: 1914
Number in sample: 14

22. VELOX stamp box with squares in corners; same POST CARD as 8; labels CORRESPONDENCE HERE and NAME AND ADDRESS HERE.

Earliest: Nov. 1907
Latest: Oct. 1910
Number in sample: 8

15.
◆ A Z O ◆
A PLACE A
Z STAMP Z
O HERE O
◆ A Z O ◆

16.
▲ A Z O ▲
A PLACE A
Z STAMP Z
O HERE O
▲ A Z O ▲

17.
POST CARD

21.
◆ V E L O X ◆
V PLACE V
E STAMP E
L HERE L
O O
X X
◆ V E L O X ◆

23. VELOX stamp box with upward-pointing triangles in corners; same POST CARD as 17; labels CORRESPONDENCE and ADDRESS.

Earliest: Sept. 1909
Latest: May 1910
Number in sample: 3

24. VELOX stamp box with diamonds in corners; same POST CARD as 17.

Earliest: Mar. 1910
Latest: Feb. 1917
Number in sample: 14

25. CYKO stamp box, same symbol as 2; POST CARD same as 2; label CORRESPONDENCE begins under middle of "O" of "POST"; label NAME AND ADDRESS begins under middle of "R" of "CARD" (see ill.).

Earliest: July 1907
Latest: Aug. 1907
Number in sample: 2

26. CYKO stamp box, same symbol as 2; same POST CARD and labels as 25, but CORRESPONDENCE shifted to align at left with "P" of "POST."

Earliest: Aug. 1907
Latest: Aug. 1910
Number in sample: 20

27. CYKO stamp box, same symbol as 2; same POST CARD as 2; label CORRESPONDENCE aligns at left with "P" of "POST"; label NAME AND ADDRESS begins under left side of "D" of "CARD."

Earliest: May 1909
Latest: July 1912
Number in sample: 18

28. CYKO stamp box, same symbol as 2; POST CARD similar to 2, but letters "P", "R", and "D" slightly squared (see ill.); label CORRESPONDENCE begins between "P" and "O" of "POST"; label NAME AND ADDRESS begins under middle of "R" of "CARD" (see ill.).

Earliest: July 1912
Latest: Nov. 1915
Number in sample: 13

29. CYKO stamp box, same symbol as 2; same POST CARD as 28; no labels.

Earliest: Oct. 1915
Latest: 1927
Number in sample: 6

30. No stamp box; same POST CARD as 5; labels CORRESPONDENCE and ADDRESS ONLY.

Earliest: Aug. 1908
Latest: June 1911
Number in sample: 15

31. KRUXO stamp box; hollow, flourished POST CARD (see ill.).

Earliest: Apr. 1908
Latest: Oct. 1911
Number in sample: 10

32. No stamp box; same POST CARD as 31; labels CORRESPONDENCE HERE and ADDRESS ONLY.

Earliest: May 1910
Latest: Nov. 1910
Number in sample: 6

33. No stamp box; same POST CARD as 31; labels CORRESPONDENCE HERE and FOR ADDRESS ONLY; "HERE" ends between "S" and "T" of "POST."

Earliest: Aug. 1907
Latest: Nov. 1907
Number in sample: 2

34. No stamp box; same POST CARD and labels as 33, but "HERE" ends under center of "T" of "POST."

Earliest: May 1911
Latest: March 1913
Number in sample: 6

35. No stamp box; same POST CARD as 31; labels CORRESPONDENCE and ADDRESS ONLY.

Earliest: Mar. 1913
Latest: June 1922
Number in sample: 13

25.
POST CARD
CORRESPONDENCE | NAME AND ADDRESS

28.
POST CARD
CORRESPONDENCE | NAME AND ADDRESS

31.
POST CARD

Acknowledgments

The authors wish to extend thanks to all those who helped in the creation of this book. Whether it was by generously offering time and expertise, or by allowing access to private collections, their help and cooperation have been essential to the successful completion of this volume.

We are especially grateful to the collectors, dealers, and curators who opened their collections to us and who gave invaluable advice and wisdom, among them Henry Deeks, Dr. George Miller, Dorothy Ryan, David Freund, Sam Wagstaff, Weston Naef of The Metropolitan Museum of Art, Don Preziosi, Newly West, Mrs. Nellie (C. B.) Micklea, Leah Schnall, Gary Wright, John Kaduk, Marion Perkins, William Peterson, José Rodriguez, Rusty Kane, Ron Menchine, Grace Watts, Bernie Stadtmiller, John and Sandy Millns, Jim Morrison, Joan Bursten, Jan and Larry Malis, Ove Braskerud, Gertrude Briggs, Myrta Hall, Daisy and Dierdre Schaeffer, Rose Mary Green, Louise Heiser, Iris Hoffman, Frank Ryan, Ben Shiffrin, and Jewell Zarvitch.

Special thanks are also due to the many individuals who helped in various aspects of the research, most notably Donald C. Ryon of the Eastman Kodak Company, Jack Boucher, Frederick Fried, Arnold R. Pilling, Mrs. Thomas Mayhill, John R. Burlinson, Eric Brus, and Elli Landon of the Oklahoma Historical Society.

For guidance at critical junctures in the project we appreciate the insights of David Smith and Eleanor Caponigro.

For advice and assistance in the editing and production of the book we are grateful to Isabella Dubow, Polly Cone, Steve and Harold Jaques of Village Craftsmen, and Sam and Ed Goldman of Publishers Book Bindery.

PRAIRIE FIRES AND PAPER MOONS
has been set in a film version of Trump Medieval, a
typeface designed by Professor Georg Trump in the
mid-1950s and cast by the C. E. Weber
Typefoundry of Stuttgart, West Germany. The
roman letter forms of Trump Medieval are based on
classical prototypes, but have been interpreted by
Professor Trump in a distinctly modern style. The
italic letter forms are more of a sloped roman than a
true italic in design, a characteristic shared by many
contemporary typefaces. The result is a modern
and distinguished type, notable both for its
legibility and versatility.

This book was composed by DEKR Corporation,
Woburn, Massachusetts, printed by Village
Craftsmen, Rosemont, New Jersey, and bound by
Publishers Book Bindery, Long Island City, New
York. The paper is Warren's Lustro Offset
Enamel, an entirely acid-free sheet.